The lost keys

Story by Jenny Giles   Illustrations by Isabel Lowe

Rachel and Sam walked to the car with Mom and Dad.
Dad looked in his pockets for the keys.

"Please open the car, Dad," said Rachel.

Dad looked in his pockets again.
"Sorry," he said. "I can't find the keys."

"Oh, dear," said Mom.
"We will have to go back
and look on the beach."

"**Oh, no!**" said Sam and Rachel.

They all went back to the beach,
looking for the keys on the way.

"Where did we sit?" said Mom.

"I can't see my sand castle," said Rachel.

"I can," said Sam. "Look!

This little hill was your castle."

"It looks funny now," said Rachel.

"The waves are splashing over it."

They looked for the keys

in the sand.

Then Rachel cried,
"We won't find the keys
in all this sand!"

"No," said Sam,
"and we can't go home!"

The waves came up to Rachel's feet.

Rachel splashed in the waves.

They ran over her feet,

and then back again.

She looked down at the wet sand.

Then she shouted, "I can see the keys!

They are here by my feet!"

"Rachel has the keys!" shouted Sam. "Now we can get into the car and go home."

"That was lucky!" said Mom. "Clever Rachel!"

"Here you are, Dad," said Rachel.

"No," laughed Dad.

"**You** can take the keys back to the car!"